# The Economics
# of Innocent Fraud

TRUTH FOR OUR TIME

JOHN KENNETH GALBRAITH

# The Economics of Innocent Fraud

TRUTH FOR OUR TIME

ALLEN LANE
*an imprint of*
PENGUIN BOOKS

ALLEN LANE

Published by the Penguin Group

Penguin Books Ltd, 80 Strand, London WC2R ORL, England
Penguin Group (USA) Inc., 375 Hudson Street, New York, New York 10014, USA
Penguin Books Australia Ltd, 250 Camberwell Road, Camberwell, Victoria 3124, Australia
Penguin Books Canada Ltd, 10 Alcorn Avenue, Toronto, Ontario, Canada M4V 3B2
Penguin Books India (P) Ltd, 11 Community Centre, Panchsheel Park, New Delhi – 110 017, India
Penguin Group (NZ), cnr Airborne and Rosedale Roads, Albany, Auckland 1310, New Zealand
Penguin Books (South Africa) (Pty) Ltd, 24 Sturdee Avenue, Rosebank 2196, South Africa

Penguin Books Ltd, Registered Offices: 80 Strand, London WC2R ORL, England

www.penguin.com

First published in the United States of America by Houghton Mifflin Books 2004
First published in Great Britain by Allen Lane 2004

1

Copyright © John Kenneth Galbraith, 2004

The moral right of the author has been asserted

The quotation from John Maynard Keynes is drawn from "Economic Possibilities for
our Grandchildren," in *Essays in Persuasion* (New York: St. Martin's Press, 1972), p. 321.

Set in 11.25/15.5 pt Linotype Sabon
Typeset by Rowland Phototypesetting Ltd, Bury St Edmunds, Suffolk

Printed in Great Britain by Clays Ltd, St Ives plc

A CIP catalogue record for this book is available from the British Library

ISBN 0-7139-9820-2

FOR SYLVIA BALDWIN

*charming and greatly competent*
*bridge between author*
*and book*

# Contents

# Introduction and a Personal Note

For some seventy years my working life has been concerned with economics, along with not infrequent departures to public and political service that had an economic aspect and one tour in journalism. During that time I have learned that to be right and useful, one must accept a continuing divergence between approved belief—what I have elsewhere called conventional wisdom—and the reality. And in the end, not surprisingly, it is the reality that counts. This small book is the result of many years of encountering, valuing and using this distinction, and it is my conclusion that reality is more obscured by social or habitual preference and personal or group pecuniary advantage in economics and politics than in any other subject. Nothing has more captured my thought, and what follows is a considered view of this difference.

A lesser point: Central to my argument here is the dominant role in the modern economic society of the corporation and of the passage of power in that entity from its owners, the stockholders, now more graciously called investors, to the management. Such is the dynamic of corporate life. Management must prevail.

As I was working on these pages, there came the great breakout in corporate power and theft with the unanticipated support of cooperative and corrupt accounting. Enron I had noticed as an example of my case; there were to be more in the headlines. Perhaps I should have been grateful; there are few times when an author can have such affirmation of what he or she has written. The corporate scandals, as they are now called, dominated the news because of exceptionally competent and detailed reporting. I forgo repetition here. I do, however, make reference to the restraints to which managerial authority must now be subject, but these are a small part of the story. More to be told is of the longer and larger departure from reality of approved and conditioned belief in the economic world.

Dealt with in this essay is how, out of the pecuniary and political pressures and fashions of the time, economics and larger economic and political systems cultivate their own version of truth. This last has no necessary relation to reality. No one is especially at fault; what it is convenient to believe is greatly preferred. This is something of which all who have studied economics, all who are now students and all who have some interest in economic and political life should be aware. It is what serves, or is not adverse to, influential economic, political and social interest.

Most progenitors of what I here intend to identify as innocent fraud are not deliberately in its service. They are unaware of how their views are shaped, how they are had. No clear legal question is involved. Response comes not from violation of law but from personal and social belief. There is no serious sense of guilt; more likely, there is self-approval.

This essay is not a totally solemn exercise. A marked enjoyment can be found in identifying self-serving belief and contrived nonsense. So it has been for the author and so he hopes it will be for the reader.

# I

# The Nature of
# Innocent Fraud

This treatise must, at the outset, contend with a seeming and severe contradiction: How can fraud be innocent? How can innocence be fraudulent? The answer is of no slight significance, for innocent, lawful fraud has an undoubted role in private life and public discourse. However, by neither those so believing nor those so guiding is there spoken recognition of that fact. There is, to emphasize, no sense of guilt or responsibility.

Some of this fraud derives from traditional economics and its teaching and some from the ritual views of economic life. These can strongly support individual and group interest, particularly, as might be expected, that of the more fortunate, articulate and politically prominent in the larger community, and can achieve the respectability and authority of everyday knowledge. This is not the contrivance of any individual or group but represents the natural, even righteous view of what best serves personal or larger interest.

An articulate community, liberal in the United States, social democratic or socialist in Europe and Japan, does ascribe economic or other motive to the interest-serving view. This can be quite wrong. What rewards particular interest may reflect only a normal tendency to self-benefiting expression and action.

As I have indicated, most of this extended essay has to do with economic matters. The reason, as I've also said, is a lifetime, and by common statistical standards rather more, of teaching, writing, discussing economics and on occasion directing economic action. The discussion has extended to the distinguished economic figures of the time, including those encountered during my term as president of the American Economic Association. Economics has been large in my life.

What I have read, heard, taught, was, I trust, well motivated. But there is always popular error. What prevails in real life is not the reality but the current fashion and the pecuniary interest. So compelling is this that, as the next chapter tells, even the every-day characterization of the economic system has been affected. When capitalism, the historic reference, ceased to be acceptable, the system was renamed. The new term was benign but without meaning. To this I now turn.

# 2

# The Renaming of
# the System

The economic system that is common to all the economically advanced countries of the world and in more
diffuse form to others—the exceptions being North
Korea, Cuba and, in reference but not in reality,
China—accords ultimate economic authority to those
in control of the relevant plant, equipment, land and
supporting financial resources. Once owners were in
charge; now firms above a certain size and with tasks at
a high level of complexity have management. Managers,
as will later be emphasized, not the owners of capital,
are the effective power in the modern enterprise. For
this reason and because the term "capitalism" evokes
a sometimes sour history, the name is in decline. In
the reputable expression of economists, business spokes-
men, careful political orators and some journalists, it is
now "the Market System." The word "capitalism" is
still heard but not often from acute and articulate
defenders of the system.

*

There is no serious doubt as to what brought the change. Capitalism emerged in Europe from the merchant era with the manufacture, buying, selling and transport of goods along with the rendering of services. Then came the industrialists, with power and prestige given by ownership, direct or indirect, and workers who suffered from their undoubted bargaining weakness—life as the alternative to often painful toil—and the resulting oppression. Marx and Engels, in some of history's most influential prose, outlined the prospect and the promise of revolution. At the end of World War I, in Russia and on its borders, the threat became the reality. Especially in Europe, the word "capitalism" affirmed too stridently this power of ownership and the magnitude of worker and larger subjugation. So came the more than plausible possibility of revolution.

In the United States, in the late nineteenth century, capitalism had a different but also negative connotation. Here it was not in the workers alone that it cultivated an adverse reaction. It also, in important measure, affected the public at large. It meant price, cost exploitation. Such was the response to the monopoly or near monopoly by John D. Rockefeller of the supply of oil, a product widely needed for illumination and other household purposes, of steel by Carnegie and tobacco by Duke. There was also the diverse power of the railroad magnates and of J. P. Morgan and his counterparts in banking and finance. In 1907, the seeming danger of widespread bankruptcy in Wall Street led to the belief that capitalism was not only exploitative but, with larger effect, self-destructive.

Beginning in the early years of the twentieth century came the American reaction in a broad thrust of legislation. The Sherman Antitrust Act sought to prevent and to punish monopolistic abuse. The Federal Reserve System was established in 1913 as a restraining force on the financial community. During Woodrow Wilson's presidency the Federal Trade Commission was introduced, with an impressive regulatory role. So negative had become the reputation of capitalism that Republicans joined and sometimes led Democrats in attempts to correct its abuses. In Europe the word "capitalism" had evoked revolution; in the United States it brought legislation, adverse judicial decisions and regulation.

There was more. During World War I, sophisticated thought, extending to belief, held that the source of the conflict and its mass death and destruction had been the rivalry between the great arms and steel combines of France and Germany. In back of the slaughter were those who, for profit, made the guns.

Later, and more destructive to the reputation of capitalism in the United States, was the visibly insane Florida real estate speculation, the rising corporate and industrial voice and, most important, the stock market explosion of the late 1920s. Then came the world-resonating crash of 1929 and, for ten long years, the Great Depression. Capitalism all too obviously did not work. So denoted, it was unacceptable.

There followed a determined search for a benign alternative name. "Free Enterprise" had a trial in the United States. It didn't take. Freedom, meaning for enterprise decisions, was not reassuring. In Europe there was "Social Democracy"—capitalism and socialism in a companionate mix. In the United States, however, socialism was (as it remains) unacceptable. In the next years reference was to the New Deal; this, however, was too clearly identified with Franklin D. Roosevelt and his cohorts. So in reasonably learned expression there came "the market system." There was no adverse history here, in fact no history at all. It would have been hard, indeed, to find a more meaningless designation— this a reason for the choice.

Markets have been important in human existence at least since the invention of coinage, commonly ascribed to the Lydians in the eighth century B.C. A respectable span of time. In all countries, including the former Soviet Union, as also in what is still by some called Communist China, they had a major role.

In the conventional economic instruction of the past, the market had special identification with consumer sovereignty—with the controlling power of the consumer in deciding what would be produced, bought and sold. Here, it was said, was the final authority to which the producing firm, the capitalist, was amply subordinate. Economic democracy, however, was too contrived to last, even in the textbooks.

Product innovation and modification is a major economic function, and no significant manufacturer introduces a new product without cultivating the consumer demand for it. Or forgoes efforts to influence and sustain the demand for an existing product. Here enters the world of advertising and salesmanship, of television, of consumer manipulation. Thus an impairment of consumer and market sovereignty.

In the real world, the producing firm and the industry go far to set the prices and establish the demand, employing to this end monopoly, oligopoly, product design and differentiation, advertising, other sales and trade promotion. This is recognized even in the orthodox economic view. Reference to the market system as a benign alternative to capitalism is a bland, meaningless disguise of the deeper corporate reality— of producer power extending to influence over, even control of, consumer demand. This, however, cannot be said. It is without emphasis in contemporary economic discussion and instruction.

So it is of the market system we teach the young. It is of this, as I've said, that sophisticated political leaders, compatible journalists and many scholars speak. No individual or firm is thus dominant. No economic power is evoked. There is nothing here from

Marx or Engels. There is only the impersonal market, a not wholly innocent fraud.

A historical connection does exist, one that should not be passed over. "Capitalism" in its time was not only the accepted designation of the economic system but the identification of those who exercised economic and therewith political authority. There was merchant capitalism, industrial capitalism, finance capitalism. These terms still have use: They create a small barrier to the complete renaming of the system even as it appears in history. One cannot speak of Venice, the supreme example of merchant capitalism, as having had a market system. Reference to the Industrial Revolution still celebrates the birth and power of industrial capitalism. In the modern financial world, allusion to capitalism has never been fully eliminated; wealth, capital, too visibly empowers. But no one can doubt that the renaming of the system, the escape from the unacceptable term "capitalism," has been somewhat successful.

Reference to a market system is, to repeat, without meaning, erroneous, bland, benign. It emerged from the desire for protection from the unsavory experience of capitalist power and, as noted, the legacy of Marx, Engels and their devout and exceptionally articulate disciples. No individual firm, no individual capitalist, is now thought to have power; that the market is subject to skilled and comprehensive management is unmentioned even in most economic teaching. Here the fraud.

Another name for the system does come persuasively to the eye and ear: "the Corporate System." None can doubt that the modern corporation is a dominant force in the present-day economy, and certainly so in the United States. Nonetheless, allusions to it are used with caution or not at all. Sensitive friends and beneficiaries of the system do not wish to assign definitive authority to the corporation. Better the benign reference to the market.

# 3

# The Economics of
# Accommodation

In the age of admitted capitalism there came a socially modifying reference. That was to the ultimate economic authority: consumer choice as to expenditure, meaning consumer sovereignty. Here the power of the public at large: economic democracy exercised by the market. This benign force, however, was not total. There could be monopoly of something essential for life or the enjoyment of life, and here there was no consumer choice. The monopolist had authority over his customers, and it extended over workers with no other job opportunity. Especially in the United States, monopoly was a major issue in economic and political thought.

With economic development, expanding incomes, more diverse consumption and, notably, new sources of supply, monopoly power and the concern therewith diminished. In the United States the antimonopoly laws, called the antitrust acts, were at one time a central political preoccupation, a valued source of legal employment and a modestly remunerative subject of university economic teaching. This I personally recall with gratitude; it was one of my early areas of instruction. All this is now much less important in both academic and general public concern. A recent prosecution of Microsoft, the great computer-driven enterprise, was a serious matter mainly to those on trial or those there serving. The phrase "monopoly capitalism," once in common use, has been dropped from the academic and political lexicon. The consumer is no longer subordinate to monopoly power; he or she is now sovereign or is so described.

The renaming of the economy served to affirm consumer sovereignty. In the market system the ultimate power, to repeat, is held to be with those who buy or choose not to buy; thus, with some qualifications, the ultimate power is that of the consumer. Consumer choice shapes to the demand curve. As the ballot gives authority to the citizen, so in economic life the demand curve accords authority to the consumer. In both instances there is a significant measure of fraud. With both ballot and buyer, there is a formidable, well-financed management of the public response. And so especially in the age of advertising and modern sales promotion. Here an accepted fraud, not least in academic instruction.

In politics and elections, mass persuasion by television

and by conventional oratory has an accepted effect on voter choice. For this, large sums of money are openly deployed. Directed not at voters but at consumers is a far more extensive, far more expensive, far more competent persuasion involved in management of the market. It comes from association with news and entertainment programs to win buyer support. This is a normal, even featured business cost. Here employed is the most accomplished and best-paid musical and theatrical talent. Artists who would once have sought patrons, writers who would once have sought readers, managers who were once primarily concerned with the production of goods and services, are now dedicated to shaping market response. Assumed is a high level of artistic creativity and financial outlay. Just as no mentally competent politician in the United States would contemplate running for a significant office without thought as to the requisite persuasion and its cost, so, at far greater expense, the control of consumer choice and sovereignty.

As does the voter, the buyer has the right to exercise independent choice, to opt out. This some do; they resort to a lifestyle outside the system that is thought eccentric, even slightly insane. The existence and exercise of such choice does not lessen the force of market persuasion. Economics as taught and believed lags well behind the reality in all but the business schools.

*

The concept of consumer sovereignty, to repeat, is still avowed in economic instruction and in defense generally of the economic system. There are still the curves and the equations. Once, after describing the reality, I was sought out for severe professional economic criticism. Advertising and salesmanship were of atmospheric irrelevance. The demand curve featured the truth; the consumer ruled. I was sternly and repeatedly reminded that even the all-powerful Ford Motor Company had failed to persuade consumers to buy an oddly shaped vehicle named for a Ford descendant—the Edsel. Here was proof of consumer sovereignty; not even a Ford could prevail.

Belief in a market economy in which the consumer is sovereign is one of our most pervasive forms of fraud. Let no one try to sell without consumer management, control.

As power over the innovation, manufacture and sale of goods and services has passed to the producer and away from the consumer, the aggregate of this production has become the prime test of social achievement. Economic and larger social advance is measured by the increase in the total production of all goods and services—in the United States what is called the Gross Domestic Product (the GDP).

There are undoubtedly rewards from an increasing GDP, for from such increase come the income, employment and products and services that sustain life and enhance its accepted enjoyments. But from the size, composition and eminence of the GDP comes also one of our socially most widespread forms of fraud. The composition of the GDP is determined not by the public at large but by those who produce its components. This, in major part, is the result of the comprehensive and talented persuasion of the economic world, including its economists. How does the GDP move? Its scale and content are extensively imposed by producers. Good performance is measured by the production of material objects and services. Not education or literature or the arts but the production of automobiles, including SUVs: Here is the modern measure of economic and therewith social achievement.

The best of the human past is the artistic, literary, religious and scientific accomplishments that emerged from societies where they were the measure of success. The art of Florence, the wonderful civic creation that is Venice, William Shakespeare, Richard Wagner and Charles Darwin, all came from communities with a very low Gross Domestic Product. It was their good fortune that they were free from the constraints of salesmanship and managed public response. Today it is only in the protected cultural, artistic, educational and scientific aspects of life that we have more compelling tests of human achievement than money.

There are no absolutes here. We do cultivate and

celebrate the arts, the sciences and their contributions to society and to the diverse values and enjoyments of life. The more than minimal fraud is in measuring social progress all but exclusively by the volume of producer-influenced production, the increase in the GDP.

# 4

# The Specious World
# of Work

All authors, indeed all who speak or write for a living, should be warned against a too enthusiastic sense of originality. What is not known by the author or orator may already be well recognized by the community at large or its informed part. So it is with work and the fraud therewith associated. What is identified with a sense of discovery is, in fact, widely urged and accepted.

The problem is that work is a radically different experience for different people. For many—and this is the common circumstance—it is compelled by the most basic command of life: It is what human beings must do, even suffer, to have a livelihood and its diverse components. It provides life's enjoyments and against its grave discomforts or something worse. Though often repetitive, exhausting, without any mental challenge, it is endured to have the necessities and some of the pleasures of living. Also a certain community repute. Enjoyment of life comes when working hours or the workweek is over. Then and then only is there escape from fatigue, boredom, the discipline of the machine, that of the workplace generally or of the managerial authority. It is frequently said that work is enjoyed; that common assertion is mostly applied to the feelings of others. The good worker is much celebrated; the celebration comes extensively from those who have escaped similar exertion, who are safely above the physical effort.

Here is the paradox. The word "work" embraces equally those for whom it is exhausting, boring, disagreeable, and those for whom it is a clear pleasure with no sense of the obligatory. There may be a satisfying feeling of personal importance or the acknowledged superiority of having others under one's command. "Work" describes both what is compelled and what is the source of the prestige and pay that others seek ardently and enjoy. Already fraud is evident in having the same word for both circumstances.

But this is not all. Those who most enjoy work—and this should be emphasized—are all but universally the best paid. This is accepted. Low wage scales are for those in repetitive, tedious, painful toil. Those who least need compensation for their effort, could best survive without it, are paid the most. The wages, or more precisely the salaries, bonuses and stock options, are the most munificent at the top, where work is a pleasure. This evokes no seriously adverse response.

Nor until recently did the inflated compensation and extensive perquisites of functional or nonfunctional executives lead to critical comment. That the most generous pay should be for those most enjoying their work has been fully accepted.

In the United States and, if less so, in other of the developed countries, no individuals invite as much criticism as those who escape the obligation to work. They are lazy, irresponsible, a burden—simply no good. This condemnation becomes severe when the alternative to work is public support. Nothing is publicly so unacceptable as going from work to welfare. The latter is the least reputable of all public expenditures. Even the welfare mother, a figure in social comment, is not spared; she should have worked instead of yielding to the pleasures of sex. Hailed as good are those by whom work is enjoyed. Also those who, having wealth and well-being, seize the rewards of leisure, personal friendship, public concern and expression and do not work at all.

In 1899, just before the beginning of the century recently ended, there appeared a deathless tract on these attitudes and beliefs. It was Thorstein Veblen's *The Theory of the Leisure Class*. With invented anthropology featuring a primitive tribal society came a study of the contrasting social customs of the American rich. For Veblen, the escape from work by the affluent was normal, and certainly for the wives and families of those thus favored. Most important was how they embellished their leisure—the mansions they built, the ostentatious lives they led, the social scene they inhabited.

Veblen was not inclined to understate his case; he left no doubt as to the commitment of the affluent to leisure and its diverse pleasures. His observations are now accepted. Work is thought essential for the poor; release therefrom is commendable for the rich.

The extent and depth of the fraud inherent in the word "work" is evident. However, little criticism or correction comes from scholarly precincts. Professors in all reputable universities limit their hourly teaching and seek and receive time off for research, writing or rewarding thought during sabbatical years. This escape from work, as for some it is, comes with no sense of guilt.

Just because leisure is an acceptable alternative for the affluent, it can still be morally damaging for the poor. It also costs money, public and private—for shorter workweeks, holidays. Therefore, while idleness is good for a leisure class in the United States and all advanced countries, it is commonly condemned for the poor. Social judgment is thus accommodated to personal pleasure and a favoring reward.

To repeat, those who render physical and repetitive effort are good workers. Little mention is made of the more pleasant circumstances of those who enjoy work, who are also better paid, or those who do not need to work at all.

It remained for the often perversely articulate John Maynard Keynes to cast doubt on the pleasure of toil. He quotes the words of an aged charwoman that were preserved on her tombstone. She had just been released from a lifetime of work:

> Don't mourn for me, friends,
> Don't weep for me, never,
> For I'm going to do nothing
> For ever and ever.

# 5

# The Corporation as Bureaucracy

The head of the large corporation—the chief executive, as he, or more rarely she, is called—is the product of a successful passage through the corporate world, one that requires the appropriate education, experience, mental acuity, bureaucratic agility, all in career competition. The major task, the successful command of the large corporate enterprise, is, however, far beyond the energy, expertise, experience and assured commitment of any single individual. Group effort, intelligence, specialization—a bureaucracy—is needed. Success comes from collective energy, general and specific knowledge, self-assertion, pursuit of financial reward and a well-developed ability to survive, lead, prevail. This the schools of business administration recognize; of this they seek to teach. The vital role of bureaucracy, even though almost never so designated, and success therein is unmentioned. In common discourse, bureaucracy and bureaucratic achievement exist in government, not in the corporate world.

On another feature there is also reticence. As with all bureaucracies, that of the corporation has a powerful tendency to self-enlargement. Pay is determined in substantial measure by the number of one's subordinates; life is more pleasant and more effective when thought and action are delegated to lesser ranks. Here an escape from specialized knowledge and tedious effort. Distinction is accorded above by the number of those below. How many does he (or she) have under him? So strong is the resulting force for expansion and so indifferent can it be to need that surgical action, called downsizing, is often required—a routine step toward greater efficiency and better earnings. The established bureaucratic tendency common to all great organizations inevitably produces some redundant staff that reflects changed need and uncorrected error.

The modern corporation, the reality notwithstanding, condemns the word "bureaucracy." That is for government. Corporate management, the established reference, has an activist tone. Participants in the management structure can be unnecessary, inept, self-concerned, but they are not bureaucrats. In government organization, group decision, delayed and less than competent action, is normal; here there is bureaucracy. Not in private industry. A small manifestation of mostly innocent fraud.

*

The management-controlled corporation is the center-piece of the modern economic system, but it is not all. There is small business, most often in the service of consumers. There are corporations, notably in technology and finance, where an initiator, not an owner, retains authority. And there are small-scale agriculture and small-scale retail and personal services. But the modern economic world centers on the controlling corporate organization; let no one escape the word, on bureaucracy.

It is accepted in small business, and particularly in what remains of family agriculture, that toil may be tedious. The owner labors in the enterprise; he or she is responsible for its direction and its success. The small businessman, the small retail and service enterprise, like the family farmer, are still featured in economic instruction and in political oratory. They are the economic system as classically described in the textbooks of centuries past. They are not the modern world; they sanction only a cherished tradition.

For the small retailer, Wal-Mart awaits. For the family farm, there are the massive grain and fruit enterprise and the modern large-scale meat producer. For all, there is the recurrent squeeze from price and cost to loss. The economic and social dominance of big business is, however, accepted. The continued political and social celebration of small business and of family agriculture is a mildly innocent form of fraud. Tradition, romance; not the reality.

The role of the individual innovator and owner in technological effort can have financial and other rewards. These are considerable—on occasion to the point of seeming near disaster, as in the great Silicon Valley experience of the last decades of the twentieth century. There unrecognized was, as ever, the terminal character of the small enterprise.

Talent for creation without organizational and diverse business skills is not enough. With age, retirement and imposed reality, power passes to a larger entity—to a management, to organization, to Microsoft. Or there is failure and oblivion. The names of founders may be remembered, even revered, but their onetime authority has passed to corporate organization—to a bureaucracy.

The corporate management illusion is our most sophisticated and in recent times one of our most evident forms of fraud. The derogatory word "capitalism" having been escaped, there is a valid designation that could be applicable—corporate bureaucracy. "Bureaucracy," however, is a term that, as indicated, is scrupulously avoided; "management" is the accepted reference. Ownership, the stockholder, is routinely recognized, even celebrated, but all too evidently is without any managerial role.

*

As sufficiently noted, guiding the modern large corporation is a demanding task, far exceeding the authority or ability of the most determined individual. From this comes a further transparent and not entirely harmless fraud. It is the effort to accord the owners, stockholders, shareholders, investors as variously denoted, a seeming role in the enterprise. Capitalism having given way to management *cum* bureaucracy, an appearance of relevance for owners is contrived. Here the fraud.

This fraud has accepted ceremonial aspects: One is a board of directors selected by management, fully subordinate to management but heard as the voice of the shareholders. It includes men and the necessary presence of one or two women who need only a passing knowledge of the enterprise; with rare exceptions, they are reliably acquiescent. Given a fee and some food, the directors are routinely informed by management on what has been decided or is already known. Approval is assumed, including for management compensation— compensation set by management for itself. This, not surprisingly, can be munificent. In the spring of 2001, during a period of stock market weakness, the *New York Times*, not a radical publication, ran a full page on the contrast between falling stock market prices and rising managerial rewards. The latter, including stock options (the right to buy stock at favored prices), could, on occasion, amount to some millions of dollars a year. All was routinely approved by the compliant directors.

Executives of the spectacularly bankrupt Enron were a prominent example, as were those of the reputable General Electric. Generous reward to management extends throughout modern corporate enterprise. Legal self-enrichment in the millions of dollars is a common feature of modern corporate government. This is not surprising; managers set their own compensation.

There are times when the need for economic and political understanding requires direct, openly adverse comment: Reference to corporate management compensation as something set by stockholders or their directors is a bogus article of faith. To affirm this fiction, stockholders are invited each year to the annual meeting, which, indeed, resembles a religious rite. There is ceremonial expression and, with rare exceptions, no negative response. Infidels who urge action are set aside; the management position is routinely approved. The shareholders who previously suggested some social policy or environmental concern have their proposals printed with supporting argument. These are uniformly rejected by management. The only significant recent exception has been at the meetings of the highly intelligent, socially eccentric and financially successful Berkshire Hathaway, Inc., of Omaha, Nebraska. Proposals by its stockholders are frequently accepted; some have thought this by prearrangement with management. In any case, it represents a highly exceptional tolerance on the part of the corporation.

No one should be in doubt: Shareholders—owners— and their alleged directors in any sizable enterprise are fully subordinate to the management. Though the impression of owner authority is offered, it does not, in fact, exist. An accepted fraud.

# 6

## The Corporate Power

The economic system having been renamed, the negative history of capitalism escaped, the next development in the world of innocent economic fraud has been the preservation of a routine capitalist image, this as the large corporation became the centerpiece of the modern economy. It could not, as told, be controlled by its owners—its stockholders. Its task is too diverse, too frequently requiring informed judgment. Power and responsibility must go to those adequately qualified and motivated; it must not go to those with no pecuniary sense and motivation or those so regarded. Thus has developed the dominance of the corporate management, the bureaucracy, although, as noted, it is not so designated. Power, as also sufficiently stressed, is the reward of knowledge, personal ambition, the accepted mood of command. And fully realized self-interest.

There is no novelty here. Over seventy years ago, in a

celebrated study—*The Modern Corporation and Private Property*—two noted Columbia University scholars and distinguished public figures, Adolf A. Berle, Jr., and Gardiner C. Means, broke the connection between corporate ownership and managerial control. The direction of the modern large corporation, they held, was multifaceted and demanding. So, as a very practical matter, power passed to the mentally qualified, actively participating management, and it did so irrevocably.

The belief that ownership has a final authority persisted, as it still does. At the annual meeting shareholders are provided with information on performance, earnings, managerial intention and other matters, including many that are already known. The resemblance is to a Covenanted Baptist Church service. Management authority remains unimpaired, including the setting of its own compensation in cash or stock options. In recent times, executive compensation so approved has, as noted, run into millions of dollars annually in an environment in which there is no adverse view of making money.

Here, to repeat, the basic fact of the twenty-first century—a corporate system based on the unrestrained power of self-enrichment. This does not go unnoticed. *Fortune* magazine, which is not given to criticism of the corporate culture, has featured vast management rewards despite diminishing corporate sales and earnings. It called them "the heist."

This is the most dramatic and one of the less innocent features of corporate management. It is also not surprising in an economic system where those favored have freedom to fix their own reward, a not entirely innocent fraud.

The myths of investor authority, of the serving stockholder, the ritual meetings of directors and the annual stockholder meeting persist, but no mentally viable observer of the modern corporation can escape the reality. Corporate power lies with management—a bureaucracy in control of its task and its compensation. Rewards that can verge on larceny. This is wholly evident. On frequent recent occasions, it has been referred to as the corporate scandal.

Something positive must also be said. The modern corporation has a highly serviceable role in contemporary economic life, more than that of the primitive, aggressively exploitative capitalist entities that preceded it.

These adverse tendencies must now be known, celebrated and addressed. The easy emphasis is on the error. More important is well-designed and enforced remedy.

# 7

# The Myth of the
# Two Sectors

In the United States, as in the other economically advanced countries, no reference is so common, so accepted, as that to the two sectors of the economic and political world. There is the private sector and there is the public sector. Once there were capitalism and socialism. Now, as noted, the word "capitalism" has partly left the language, and when still used, it has a mildly negative connotation. In the United States, socialism, government initiative and action, is thought deeply unacceptable. Few wish to be known as socialists. Accordingly, and benignly, all reference is to a private and a necessary public sector.

The resulting debate is entirely on specifics. Should we have publicly financed health care, assistance to the poor, retired and needful or for the cost of education, all traditionally in the private sector? Should we privatize, as it is said, other government activities? Is such public action at cost to personal freedom? In the

United States and in lesser measure in other countries, the role of the two sectors supports intense debate, the most extended and often tedious of oratory. Absent only is the reality.

The accepted distinction between the public and the private sectors has no meaning when seriously viewed. Rhetoric, not reality. A large, vital and expanding part of what is called the public sector is for all practical effect in the private sector.

In the fiscal year 2003, close to half of the total of United States government discretionary expenditure (outlay not mandated for a particular use, such as Social Security or service of the public debt) was used for military purposes—for defense, as more favorably it is commonly called. A large part was for weapons procurement or for weapons innovation and development. Nuclear-powered submarines run to billions of dollars, individual planes to tens of millions each. Similarly, if less spectacularly, other weaponry and military equipment. Such expenditure proceeds from the advocacy and influence of those involved and rewarded, even on to nuclear defense, so called.

Arms expenditure does not occur after detached analysis by the public sector as commonly understood. Much is at the initiative and with the authority of the arms industry and its political voice—the private sector. From the relevant industrial firms come proposed designs for new weapons, and to them are awarded production and profit. So also returns from the production of existing weaponry. In an impressive flow of influence and command, the weapons industry accords valued employment, management pay and profit in its political constituency, and indirectly it is a treasured source of political funds. The gratitude and the promise of political help go to Washington and to the defense budget, on to the Pentagon need and decision. And to foreign policy or, as recently in Vietnam and Iraq, to war. That the private sector moves to a dominant public-sector role is apparent. It would be better to describe it in plain language.

One has, indeed, a limited sense of originality in speaking of the myth of the two sectors. It was first and influentially identified by President Dwight D. Eisenhower in his noted warning of a military-industrial complex. Explicit was the takeover of public weapons policy by the defense industry. So the irrelevance of the common distinction between the two sectors. Truth is persuasive when it comes from a President and the most noted military figure of his time.

The myth of the two sectors and its formidable consequences is dissolved with a sense of urgent purpose but not, as I've said, of great originality. Nor is it, socially and politically, an innocent fraud.

*

In recent times the intrusion into what is called the public sector by the ostensibly private sector has become a commonplace. Management having full authority in the modern great corporation, it was natural that it would extend its role to politics and to government. Once there was the public reach of capitalism; now it is that of corporate management. At this writing, corporate managers are in close alliance with the President, the Vice President and the Secretary of Defense. Major corporate figures are also in senior positions elsewhere in the federal government; one came from the bankrupt and thieving Enron to preside over the Army.

Defense and weapons development are motivating forces in foreign policy. For some years there has also been recognized corporate control of the Treasury. And of environmental policy. And there is more, as should be expected.

The media have extensively accepted this political development. Writers of intelligence and courage have recognized the erstwhile private power that controls weapons design, the development of a missile defense and the military budget. It is understood that there is a major corporate role in economic policy. While the Pentagon is still billed as being of the public sector, few doubt the influence of corporate power in its decisions. What occurs every day is not news.

*

The blurring of the difference between the private and corporate sector and the diminishing public sector proceeds. On Sunday, October 13, 2002, the *New York Times* told of business firms moving ever closer to actual combat. No one could ask for more dramatic proof that the two sectors have become one. Here the *Times* account; it got little attention at the time. What it reported was already perhaps a commonplace:

[Corporations now provide] stand-ins for active soldiers in everything from logistical support to battlefield training . . .

Some [firms] are helping to conduct training exercises using live ammunition for American troops in Kuwait, under the code name Desert Spring . . . Others have employees who don their old uniforms to work under contract as military recruiters and instructors in R.O.T.C. classes, selecting and training the next generation of soldiers.

So the reality. In war command as in peace, the private becomes the public sector.

# 8

# The World of Finance

Now a well-recognized area of innocent fraud. And here some that is legally less than innocent. This is the world of finance—of banking, corporate finance, the securities markets, the mutual funds, organized financial guidance and advice.

The fraud begins with a controlling fact, inescapably evident but all but universally ignored. It is that the future economic performance of the economy, the passage from good times to recession or depression and back, cannot be foretold. There are more than ample predictions but no firm knowledge. All contend with a diverse combination of uncertain government action, unknown corporate and individual behavior and, in the larger world, with peace or war. Also with unforeseeable technological and other innovation and consumer and investment response. There is the variable effect of exports, imports, capital movements and corporate, public and government reaction thereto.

Thus the all-too-evident fact: The combined result of the unknown cannot be known. This is true for the economy as a whole, as also for the specific industry or firm. So the view of the economic future has always been. So it will always be.

In the economic and especially the financial world, nonetheless, prediction of the unknown and unknowable is a cherished and often well-rewarded occupation. It can be the basis, though often briefly, of a remunerative career. From it comes allegedly informed judgment as to the general economic prospect and that of the individual participating and affected enterprise. The men and women so engaged believe and are believed by others to have knowledge of the unknown; research is thought to create such knowledge. Because what is predicted is what others wish to hear and what they wish to profit or have some return from, hope or need covers reality. Thus in the financial markets we celebrate, even welcome essential error.

Shared error has also a well-protected role. It is no longer a personal matter. The financial world sustains a large, active, well-rewarded community based on compelled but seemingly sophisticated ignorance.

To repeat, those employed or self-employed who tell of the future financial performance of an industry or firm, given the unpredictable but controlling influence of the larger economy, do not know and normally do not know that they do not know. Predictions from a financial firm, Wall Street economist or financial adviser as to the economic prospect for a corporation—recession, scheduled recovery or a continuing economic boom—are thought to reflect economic and financial expertise. And there is no easy denial of an expert's foresight. Past accidental success and an ample display of charts, equations and self-confidence affirm depth of perception. Thus the fraud. Correction awaits.

Financial advice and guidance, however worthless, can be for a time financially rewarding. Then comes the overriding truth. In recent years, such has been the common experience. Technological innovation—real, predicted, contrived or imagined—was long centered on a physically commonplace part of California, world-famous as Silicon Valley. What followed was an intense and ultimately definitive manifestation of fraud, as recent comment has made clear. From once highly regarded stockbrokers and investment firms, the financial press and imaginative and mentally vulnerable newcomers came well-believed forecasts of the glowing prospects of Silicon Valley firms. So from others with a personal stake. The subject firms were enthusiastically celebrated and the progenitors further rewarded. Those making the forecasts were well paid; this was not entirely innocent. Financial gains in Silicon Valley were also derived from thoughtfully enhanced and compensated expectations.

Here another largely accepted manifestation of fraud. It occurs when a less than successful venture encounters the adverse forces of reality. The causes of reduced corporate performance have been realized. They are, invariably, the same—impersonal market forces, absent public restraints, simple theft. The universal remedy: vigorous downsizing—layoffs of those least responsible. The larger the number so released, the better regarded the financial prospect. No one is sacked, fired; instead there is a wholesome assignment to family, leisure, home enjoyments, education and career improvement. Let the remedial hardship, including for those least responsible for bad performance—those denoted as good workers—be publicly known. Brutal but determined action. A verbal fraud somewhat so recognized.

Since the above was written, attention has been accorded a specific fraud in the field of finance. It calls for special comment by one professionally associated with the world of economics. Identification of the fraud has been the contribution of the diligent attorney general of New York State, and it casts an interesting, even compelling light on research by economists in financial markets. On Wall Street, economists had not confined themselves to passive, unfavored reward.

Instead they chose to forecast what most rewarded those requesting the research. Also they indulged in well-publicized prediction that was favorable to their personal holdings—prediction molded to serve personal gain or to protect against personal loss. A blight on professional economics; a fraud close to home.

# 9

# The Elegant Escape
from Reality

I come now to our most prestigious form of fraud, our most elegant escape from reality. As sufficiently noted, the modern economic system is unpredictable in its movement from good times to bad and then eventually from bad to good. Boom, bubble and inflation go on to declining production, rising unemployment, reduced earnings, stable but lower prices. Then, in time, to a revival—to higher employment, greater earnings, talk if not the reality of inflation. To limit unemployment and recession in the United States and the risk of inflation, the remedial entity is the Federal Reserve System, the central bank. For many years (with more to come) this has been under the direction from Washington of a greatly respected chairman, Mr. Alan Greenspan. The institution and its leader are the ordained answer to both boom and inflation and recession or depression with its lower production, financial and economic contraction, distress and reduced employment. Quiet measures enforced by the Federal Reserve are thought to be the best approved, best accepted of economic actions. They are also manifestly ineffective. They do not accomplish what they are presumed to accomplish. Recession and unemployment or boom and inflation continue. Here is our most cherished and, on examination, most evident form of fraud.

The false and favorable reputation of the Federal Reserve has a strong foundation: There is the power and prestige of banks and bankers and the magic accorded to money. These stand behind and support the Federal Reserve and its member—that is, belonging— banks. If in recession the interest rate is lowered by the central bank, the member banks are counted on to pass the lower rate along to their customers, thus encouraging them to borrow. Producers will then produce goods and services, buy the plant and machinery they can now afford and from which they can now make money, and consumption paid for by cheaper loans will expand. The economy will respond, the recession will end. If then there is a boom and threat of inflation, a higher cost of borrowing initiated also by the Federal Reserve and imposed on its lending to member banks will raise interest rates. This will restrain business investment and consumer borrowing, counter the excess of optimism, level off prices and thus insure against inflation.

The difficulty is that this highly plausible, wholly agreeable process exists only in well-established economic belief and not in real life. The belief depends on the seemingly persuasive theory and on neither reality nor practical experience. Business firms borrow when they can make money and not because interest rates are low. As this is written, in 2003, during a recession, the lending rate of the Federal Reserve has been reduced roughly a dozen times in the recent past. These reductions have been strongly approved as the wise and effective response to the recession, so acknowledged in both popular and learned comment. How good this simple, painless design, free from politics and in the hands of responsible and respected professional and public figures free from political taint. No disagreeable debate, no pointless controversy. Also, and uncelebrated, no economic effect.

Especially as regards recession, hope always awaits the next Federal Reserve meeting. There is then promise, prediction and ultimately no result. On no economic matter does history more reliably repeat itself. One should, however, be gentle. The action is reputable and well regulated; there is general agreement by the participants and approval from the financial world; it is just that nothing perceptible occurs. Recovery comes, but not in any visible way, from Federal Reserve action. Housing improves as mortgage rates decline. Elsewhere there is painful indifference. Interest rates are a detail when sales are bad. Firms do not borrow and expand output that cannot be sold.

*

Since 1913, when the Federal Reserve came fully into existence, it has had a record against inflation and notably against recession of deep and unrelieved inconsequence. In World War I, prices doubled in the course of the two years the United States was at war. No remedy came from the new and magical central bank. In the 1920s, in Florida and then disastrously on Wall Street, came unbridled and, in its aftermath, deeply damaging speculation. There was no effective restraint from the Federal Reserve. Then for a decade the Great Depression, and once more no curative action from Washington and the Fed. Informed debate, no result. Deflation and depression persisted.

During World War II, because of the previous wartime experience, inflation was greatly feared. In the event, however, it was closely controlled and no seriously unpleasant memory remains. Historians pass the problem by. This agreeable outcome was more than slightly because, acting on what had earlier occurred, there was no reliance on the Federal Reserve. Economic policy in this truly difficult time could not be based on hope or mythology. As one principally responsible for limiting inflation in those years (I was the deputy administrator in charge of price policy in the Office of Price Administration and thus immediately concerned with the action against inflation), I shared the belief that the Federal Reserve was irrelevant. So it was.

In the decades since World War II, there have been

lesser threats of inflation and recession. The Federal Reserve, after learned and intense discussion, has acted. There have been well-voiced approval, optimistic prediction and no effect.

Such are Chairman Greenspan's public skills, such is the ingrained faith in any action involving money, that the Fed, as affectionately it is called, will receive credit if and when there is full recovery. The fact will remain: When times are good, higher interest rates do not slow business investment. They do not much matter; the larger prospect for profit is what counts. And in recession or depression, the controlling factor is the poor earnings prospect. At the lower interest rates, housing mortgages are refinanced; the total amount of money so released to debtors is relatively small and some may be saved. Widespread economic effect is absent or insignificant.

In restraining inflation, or what seems such purpose, the Federal Reserve must be especially cautious; it cannot be thought to be in conflict with economic well-being. If and when recession returns, the defining forces, as later noted, will be the consumer spending and industry investment so called forth. On these, what follows from central-bank action is minimal. Business firms respond to diminishing sales. Here the Federal Reserve has no decisive role. Only in innocence does it control general consumer and business spending.

Nonetheless, it is thought good to have an

uncontroversial, politically neutral institution headed as in all recent times by an informed, confident and respected figure of no slight theatrical talent. How agreeable decisions taken in reputable surroundings beneath the portraits of the financially celebrated of the past. It is thus that economic policy should be decided. That nothing important results is overlooked. The belief that anything as complex, as diverse and by its nature personally as important as money can be guided by well-discussed but painless decisions emanating from a pleasant, unobtrusive building in the nation's capital belongs not to the real world but to that of hope and imagination. Here our most implausible and most cherished escape from reality. No one should deny those participating their innocently acquired prestige, their sense of personal competence, their largely innocent enjoyment of what in economic effect is a well-established fraud. Perhaps we should let their ineffective role be accepted and forgiven.

# IO

# The End to Corporate Innocence

On one matter in these pages there will be agreement, but also no valid claim to originality. That is the major economic role of the modern great corporation and therewith of its management. There is a strong corporate presence and initiative in what is still called the public sector and great public influence from erstwhile corporate managers. Management having the essential dominant role in the modern large corporation, the role of the stockholders has become ceremonial and is given largely by the calendar. Celebrated recently, with some surprise and shock, has been the managerial thrust for power and self-enrichment. Executives of Enron, WorldCom, Tyco and others became the focus of widely publicized criticism, even outrage. Joining the language came the reference to corporate scandals. Avoided only was mention of the compelling opportunity for enrichment that had been accorded the managers of the modern corporate enterprise, and this in a world that approves of self-enrichment as the basic reward for economic merit.

Great firms, particularly in energy and mass communications but not so confined, came to dominate the news. In all cases, the situation was the same, as was the result. Management was in full control. Ownership was irrelevant; some auditors were compliant. Stock options added participant wealth and slightly concealed the take.

The least expected contribution to the adverse and even criminal activity was the corrupt accounting just mentioned. This provided cover for devious actions that extended to outright theft. Individuals of inquiring mind had long regarded accounting as both competent and honest. Over a professional lifetime in economics, as a teacher, author and sometime public official, and from some personal interest, I have read through dozens, perhaps hundreds of corporate financial statements. That some were a disguise for quiet larceny did not cross my mind.

The corporate scandals and especially the associated publicity have led to discussion or appropriate regulation and some action—to positive steps to insure accounting honesty and some proposed remedies, as required, to counter management and lesser corporate fraud. Attention has been drawn to unduly compliant public officials, including those on the essential Securities and Exchange Commission. One obvious result has been well-justified doubt as to the quality of much present regulatory effort. There is no question but that corporate influence extends to the regulators. It is less easy to defend corporate behavior in the face of a negative public view. Needed is independent, honest, professionally competent regulation—again, a difficult thing to achieve in a world of corporate dominance. This last must be recognized and countered. There is no alternative to effective supervision. Management behavior can also be improved by thoughtful contemplation of the wholly real possibility of less than agreeable incarceration.

More important, it must be seen that good corporate behavior with effective regulation is greatly in the public interest. Managerial misappropriation is not. This must be understood not as oratory, not as threat, but as reality. No one should suppose that supervisory participation by directors and shareholders is sufficient. Remedy and safeguard must have the force of law.

Management authority, its abuse and personal enrichment, will continue. The prime hope must be full recognition by the public and by public authority of the opportunity it affords for socially undesirable behavior. Accordingly, there must be surveillance of the reputable enterprise and general attention to managerial self-reward. This is in the interest of both the public and the corporate world. The corporation, to repeat, is an essential feature of modern economic life. We must have it. It must conform, however, to accepted standards and requisite public restraints. Freedom for beneficial economic action is necessary; freedom should not be a cover for either legal or illegal misappropriation of income or wealth. Corporate management must have authority for action but not for seemingly innocent theft. Here the most challenging and, given corporate power, the most urgent need. A society of corporate economic misadventure and crime will not usefully survive and serve. I turn to a more general matter.

# I I

# Foreign and Military Policy

The most controversial case for truth and reality emerges from the previously noted myth of the two sectors. Any expansion of the valid public sector and its social or economic support is well recognized. This the dominant corporate voice resists. Here, in the established view, is the ever-threatening government assault on private enterprise, which is condemned at the extremes of oratory as socialism. Private corporate movement into the public sector by conceded influence or activity is much less discussed or not at all. Here a compelling attitude and action of our time.

As the corporate interest moves to power in what was the public sector, it serves, predictably, the corporate interest. That is its purpose. It is most important and most clearly evident in the largest such movement, that of nominally private firms into the defense establishment, the Pentagon. From this comes a primary influence on the military budget. Also, and much more than marginally, on foreign policy, military commitment and, ultimately, military action. War. Although this is a normal and expected use of money and its power, the full effect is disguised by almost all conventional expression.

In the two world wars it was assumed that military purpose should be decisive as to foreign policy. Military allies were an essential; for this and much else, power was passed to the generals. In World War II, as I've told, I was in charge of central economic policy—control of all prices and in initial stages also of rationing. The needed action on war-related industries—steel, copper and rubber, food, other farm products, notably textiles—brought me into close touch with military need. Accommodation was assumed.

At the end of the war I was director for overall effects of the United States Strategic Bombing Survey—USBUS, as it was known. I led a large professional economic staff in assessment of the industrial and military effects of the bombing of Germany and later, less comprehensively, of Japan. In Germany the strategic bombing, that of industry, transportation and cities, was gravely disappointing. The war was not shortened. Attacks on factories that made such seemingly crucial components as ball bearings and eventually on aircraft plants were sadly useless. With plant and machinery relocation and better, more determined management, fighter aircraft production actually increased in early 1944 after major bombing. In the cities the random cruelty and death inflicted from the sky had no appreciable effect on war production or the war.

These findings were vigorously resisted by the Allied armed services, especially, needless to say, the air command, even though they were the work of the most capable and relevant scholars of the United States and Britain and were supported by German industry officials and impeccable German statistics. Also by the noted director of German arms production, Albert Speer. All our conclusions were cast aside—this, as said, the response of the air command and its public and academic allies. The latter united to arrest my appointment to a Harvard professorship and succeeded in doing so for a year.

Nor is this all. The greatest military misadventure in American history until Iraq was the war in Vietnam. In that country, to which I was sent on a fact-finding mission in the early sixties, I had a full view of military dominance as to foreign policy, a dominance that has now extended to replacement of the presumed civilian authority. In India, where I was ambassador, in Washington, where I had access to President Kennedy, and in Saigon, I developed a strongly negative view of the conflict. Later I encouraged and supported the antiwar campaign of Eugene McCarthy in 1968. His candidacy was first announced in our house in Cambridge. I was his floor manager at the chaotic

Democratic Convention in Chicago that year, and with no evident effect, I seconded his nomination.

During all this time the military establishment in Washington was in support of the war. This, indeed, was assumed. It was occupationally appropriate that both the armed services and the weapons industries should accept and endorse hostilities. To repeat, this was taken for granted. Again the spurious distinction between a private and a public sector. Here, clearly evident, the corporate interest in the rewarding contracts. Here Dwight D. Eisenhower's military-industrial complex. We do not wish to live with the reality; that does not deny that it exists. Better that it be accepted.

# 12

# The Last Word

One thing, I trust, has emerged in this book: That is the now-dominant role of the corporation and corporate management in the modern economy. Once in the United States, as told, there were capitalists. Steel by Carnegie, oil by Rockefeller, tobacco by Duke, railroads variously and often incompetently controlled by the moneyed few. Celebrated were the financial magnates, not for their economic performance but for their latent or active economic power and, not exceptionally, for their well-celebrated public good—the great foundations.

In its market position and political influence, modern corporate management, unlike the capitalist, has public acceptance. A dominant role in the military establishment, in public finance and the environment is assumed. Other public authority is also taken for granted. And, as sufficiently noted, the Gross Domestic Product with the corporate contribution thereto is the acknowledged measure of economic, even civilized success. Adverse social flaws and their effect do, however, require attention.

One, as just observed, is the way the corporate power has shaped the public purpose to its own ability and need. It ordains that social success is more automobiles, more television sets, more diverse apparel, a greater volume of all other consumer goods. Also more and more lethal weaponry. Here is the measure of human achievement. Negative social effects—pollution, destruction of the landscape, the unprotected health of the citizenry, the threat of military action and death—do not count as such. When measuring achievement, the good and the disastrous can be combined.

The corporate appropriation of public initiative and authority is unpleasantly visible as regards the environmental effect, dangerous as regards military and foreign policy. Wars are, one cannot doubt, a major modern threat to civilized existence, and corporate commitment to weapons procurement and use nurtures and supports this threat. It accords legitimacy and even heroic virtue to devastation and death. On this a later word.

It must be accepted—the evident has its truth—that power in the modern great corporation belongs to the management. The board of directors is an amiable entity, meeting with self-approval and fraternal respect but fully subordinate to the real power of the managers. The relationship somewhat resembles that of an honorary degree recipient to a member of a university faculty. As told, a commonplace of corporate authority is the setting of management compensation, this in a situation where the extent of such reward is a measure of achievement. It can also, as spectacular recent history has shown, be carried wonderfully to excess.

Damage to the corporate world itself—to the view of corporate achievement and reputation—is always possible. Within the economy there is movement from public acceptance of the corporate system to its being seen as a military threat to all human life. Also there are here unemployment and economic discontent, a contributing factor to recession or the more fearsome depression.

As sufficiently said, the performance of the corporate system, specifically the sequence and duration of boom and recession, cannot be foreseen. The causes in all their varied effect cannot be known in advance. No feature of the modern economy is more remarkable than the volume of corporate and personal revenue that comes from the marketing of the unknown. A reputation for persuasive nonknowledge and the diverse nontalent that is brought to bear is a less than innocent aspect of modern economic life.

I have here resisted describing the unknown. Curative or damaging action can, on the other hand, be identified.

Specifically, there is no indication that tax relief as recently urged and adopted had an ameliorative effect on recession. Corporate investment, production and employment were held to respond to the after-tax income promised to corporations, to corporate management and financially well situated stockholders in the form of relief from taxation of the dividend income of the rich. All managements believe, as do economists, that money accruing to them serves a larger public good. There was, however, no certainty that income accruing to the corporate affluent would have a positive effect—would be spent. For the corporate elite, tax reduction enhances income that is already more than ample. Even for the affluent, enough is enough. Additional income from tax reduction is not reliably spent, and so it can be without effect.

There is more. The one wholly reliable remedy for recession is a solid flow of consumer demand. Failure in such a flow is a recession. In the United States, especially with stagnation and recession, the lower-income citizen has an acute need for education, health care, a basic family income in one form or another. State and local governments, under the pressure of enhanced demand, cut social outlays. This is particularly evident as this is written. The overall effect has been reduced personal and family income and well-being—recession without effective curative action. So at this writing.

In its compelling history, economic policy has often been at odds with economic well-being. And it can be without clear effect. There can be money for those who would not spend, privation for those who would. Recession independent of remedial public policy. Improvement without any obvious effective action.

It would be pleasant to offer a more affirmative note. In the economic world there is established belief, and this can support adverse or positive economic policy. A recession calls for a reliable flow of purchasing power, especially for the needful, who will spend. Here there is an assured effect, but it is resisted as unserviceable compassion. What best serves managerial pecuniary interest can be so dismissed. There can be pecuniary reward, most often tax relief, for the socially influential. In the absence of need, it may not be spent. The needful are denied the money they will surely spend; the affluent are accorded the income they will almost certainly save.

A final word. We cherish the progress in civilization since biblical times and long before. But there is a needed and, indeed, accepted qualification. As I write, the United States and Britain are in the bitter aftermath of a war in Iraq. We are accepting programmed death for the young and random slaughter for men and women of all ages. So, overwhelmingly, it was in World Wars I and II. So more selectively since, and still at this writing in Iraq. Civilized life, as it is called, is a great white tower celebrating human achievements, but at the top there is permanently a large black cloud. Human progress dominated by unimaginable cruelty and death.

I leave the reader with the sadly relevant fact: Civilization has made great strides over the centuries in science, health care, the arts and most, if not all, economic well-being. But also it has given a privileged position to the development of weapons and the threat and reality of war. Mass slaughter has become the ultimate civilized achievement.

The facts of war are inescapable—death and random cruelty, suspension of civilized values, a disordered aftermath. Thus the human condition and prospect as now supremely evident. The economic and social problems here described, as also mass poverty and starvation, can, with thought and action, be addressed. So they have already been. War remains the decisive human failure.

# Online access to the facts, figures and faces behind the headlines.

**The Financial Times is giving Penguin readers the chance to SAVE OVER 40% on subscription to FT.com – the world's leading business website.**

Subscribe today and benefit from:

- **Instant access:** Search the entire FT archive, plus in-depth company information, with a tool that gives you relevant results fast.

- **Instant updates:** Give us any company names or topics and we'll email you relevant news as soon as it's published.

- **Instant analysis:** Get behind the headlines to the real story with the FT's informed, rapid-response analysis.

You'll also gain access to the full library of FT reports, an overnight preview of tomorrow's FT newspaper, sections devoted to industries, and access to our PDA service.

Claim your special Penguin price today and become an instant expert with the world's leading business website.

**Visit www.ft.com/penguinreader**

FT.com
FINANCIAL TIMES